A Biblical Response to Liberal Christianity

CONCORDIA PUBLISHING HOUSE · SAINT LOUIS

3558 S. Jefferson Ave., St. Louis, MO 63118-3968
1-800-325-3040 • cph.org

Written by Alfonso Espinosa

Manufactured in the United States of America

1 2 3 4 5 6 7 8 9 10 31 30 29 28 27 26 25 24 23 22

WHAT IS LIBERAL CHRISTIANITY?

Well, this is an interesting combination of words: *liberal* and *Christianity*. What is up with qualifying *Christianity* with *liberal*? The word *liberal* gets a lot of press. In the political arena, it is contrasted with *conservative*, and all kinds of connotations are attached to each label. Let's back up and look at the academic origins of the word *liberal* to see how it eventually affected the way people talk about God.

Initially used in academia, the word *liberal* represented the good goal to practice "liberty of thought," in the sense of making education as thorough and complete as possible. This was consistent with referring to institutions of higher education as universities. Notice what word is contained within the word *university*: *universe*. This was a place where all academic disciplines converged to provide the most complete exposure to knowledge. The person equipped this way was considered educated.

If a university offered a liberal arts program, one could enroll in it and count on acquiring a working knowledge of science, mathematics, history, philosophy, literature, and even theology (or at least religion or religious studies). In this context, "liberal" is something to be admired.

With that background, the phrase "liberal Christianity" might seem positive, as though it means to uphold the Christian faith with maximal knowledge. Could there be a more praiseworthy goal? First, start with as much knowledge about the world and universe as possible; then, hold to the wonderful Christian faith that advocates the greatest commandments of God to love Him and to love fellow human beings (Matthew 22:37–39).

Notice, however, that the description above highlights the ethical or moral aspect of the commandment to love God and neighbor; it doesn't mention the rest of the Bible and what God reveals there. Liberal Christianity emphasizes the moralistic and therapeutic at the expense of upholding the rest of Scripture, especially the miraculous. In other words, liberal Christianity (also referred to as progressive Christianity or modern American Christianity) is a feel-good religion that affirms people regardless of what they believe in or practice while permitting the world's knowledge to qualify the rest of Scripture. No wonder liberal Christianity is so popular!

This contrasts with biblical Christianity. Biblical—that is, actual—Christianity is about more than morality. Biblical Christianity stresses what the Bible reveals about who Jesus is and what Jesus did, does, and will do to save humanity from sin, death, and the real powers of darkness.

FROM CENTRAL TO EQUAL

Until the early 1800s, biblical Christianity was known as the "queen of the sciences" among all academic disciplines. One could not properly pursue other disciplines without the foundation of biblical Christianity. For example, biblical Christianity's article of biblical creation set the stage for the scientific method. The world's existence is not random but specifically designed, so that one may observe its unique characteristics. The scientific method begins by observing this one-of-a-kind creation. Furthermore, because the natural order is created, it is not in itself divine. As a result, humans are permitted to experiment on what has been created.

In other words, biblical Christianity as revealed in the Word of God was the central discipline: the single most important source of knowledge and truth. Everything Holy Scripture taught was considered true. From this truth—whole and unqualified—all other disciplines could properly approach the world God created and the life God graciously bestows.

But over time, biblical Christianity lost that central position and instead came to hold an equal or even inferior position among the other disciplines. Whereas Christianity had once influenced our understanding of all other fields, now those other fields could also influence the understanding of Christianity. And while fields such as linguistics, geography, or history may genuinely help us to understand Scripture, we must recognize the shift that occurred: Christianity was demoted from the primary sphere of influence.

GOD'S WORD IS NO LONGER PRIMARY

So what happens when Christianity becomes liberal Christianity, when it becomes just one discipline or field of knowledge among others? The main result is the growing assumption that human reason is the highest authority, even above the Word of God.

Martin Luther and other faithful reformers confessed Holy Scripture as the absolute authority for what God calls us to believe, teach, and confess. Their teaching of *sola Scriptura*—Scripture alone—expresses that the Word of God is the only authoritative source that forms the confession of the Christian Church. Biblical Christianity affirms that Scripture is inspired, or "breathed out," by God (2 Timothy 3:16) and therefore inerrant (that is, without error).

However, because liberal Christianity is led mainly by human reason, it ends up denying both the inspiration and the inerrancy of God's Word. God's Word is demoted from being the primary source of truth to an inferior source, if it is even considered at all.

HISTORICAL BACKGROUND

The main problem of liberal Christianity is, in one sense, the same problem we see in Genesis 3. By listening to Satan's temptation of "Did God really say . . .?" (Genesis 3:1), Adam and Eve allowed their human reason to qualify God's Word. As soon as we do this, it becomes easy to think we can be religious while maintaining autonomy apart from God's Word, like what happened in the Book of Judges: "In those days there was no king in Israel. Everyone did what was right in his own eyes" (21:25).

After the Reformation, the cultural trends that arose from the Age of Reason (also known as the Enlightenment) in the 1700s reinforced the priority of human reason. For example, humanist philosopher David Hume argued that miracles were contrary to the laws of nature and were therefore impossible, which profoundly changed how people viewed Scripture.

Once miracles were qualified and denied, it was only a matter of time until Scripture would have to be recast and reinterpreted. A popular Enlightenment-period argument was that the disciples stole Jesus' body from the tomb and fabricated the four Gospels, making up Jesus' resurrection and the miracles He conducted during His earthly ministry so they could maintain their status as disciples.

As a result of this devastating compromise of biblical teaching, Deism became popular: the belief that there is a god (which might account for the existence of the universe), but that this god is entirely detached from creation and has no direct dealings or interactions with life on earth. This categorically denies the Bible's teaching that Jesus Christ is the Son of God who took on human flesh to save people from the power of sin and death.

Many theologians and philosophers feared that the Deist position would lead to the total collapse of Christianity, and they wanted to maintain the outstanding reputation of Jesus Christ and His teaching. In other words, they strove to maintain a kind of Christianity in the face of the developments that came through the Age of Reason.

So in the 1800s, theologians such as Albrecht Ritschl tried to combine the best of scientific and historical scholarship with what was viewed as a sincere expression of the Christian faith, creating what is now known as liberal Christianity. Ritschl advocated for the full use of all the other disciplines to rightly interpret Scripture. There was just one catch: this approach maintained the faulty Enlightenment assumptions that miracles are impossible and that the Holy Scriptures are neither inspired nor inerrant.

In Ritschl's system, and likewise in modern liberal Christianity, the miraculous accounts of the life, death, and resurrection of Jesus Christ are automatically dismissed. Still, liberal Christianity values the "religious experience" of Christianity, which includes the outstanding moral example and teachings of Jesus Christ. Rather than the redemption that biblical Christianity teaches, liberal Christianity's version of redemption is simply to discover and live the life of love that Jesus demonstrated.

Notice how liberal Christianity still maintains a connection to the name of Jesus Christ. This is why the word *Christianity* is still connected to the word *liberal* in this belief system. It is liberal because, in the final result, human reason holds authority over the Word of God, and it is Christianity because it still attempts to apply and emulate Jesus' way of life. But this removes the biblical teachings of the divinity of Christ, the devastating problem of original sin, Christ's virgin birth, His life that fulfilled the Law for poor sinners, His death that shed His blood to atone for the sins of the world, and His bodily resurrection, which defeated death for us. In other words, the "Christianity" of liberal Christianity is no longer biblical Christianity.

DIFFERENT USES OF REASON

One important point to understand is that biblical Christianity does not eliminate or avoid the use of reason. Instead, we use it in proper relation to God's Word. When reason is kept in its proper place beneath the Word of God, honoring God's Word as authoritative, then reason is good. We refer to this as the ministerial use of reason because it ministers to, or serves, the Word of God.

However, reason is used wrongly when we put it above the Word of God, as in liberal Christianity. This is called the magisterial use of reason, meaning that reason has become the master or authority. When reason is given majesty or authority over God's Word, making Holy Scripture subservient to reason, then reason is being used incorrectly.

Sometimes people claim that reason is now sanctified, or made holy, by the Word of God and that it can therefore be used equally with Holy Scripture. But making reason equally authoritative with Scripture is still a magisterial use. If reason is given equal authority, it is only a matter of time until reason is given more authority.

With this background in mind, we can engage the ideas of liberal Christianity with the truth of Scripture. The following sections will examine specific lines of thought related to liberal Christianity and provide biblical answers.

NATURAL KNOWLEDGE OF GOD

Liberal Christianity holds to one primary belief that makes it different from biblical Christianity: the rejection of miracles and the miraculous. But we can respond to this position using the natural knowledge of God.

So what is the natural knowledge of God? The natural knowledge of God is the idea that, even apart from the Bible, people have immediate ways to know that God is the Creator and is the highest authority over all people.

Romans 1 teaches that all people have a natural knowledge of God by virtue of their ability to observe creation: "For what can be known about God is plain to them, because God has shown it to them. For His invisible attributes, namely, His eternal power and divine nature, have been clearly perceived, ever since the creation of the world, in the things that have been made" (vv. 19–20). The existence of creation itself proclaims that there is a Creator, that it did not just appear from nothing but has a cause. This is the external evidence of God in our lives. Despite the arguments of humanist philosophers who try to make us doubt our perceptions, what we see around us tells us that the law of cause-and-effect must be true.

We may also present this position without citing the Bible, using a syllogism (a type of deductive reasoning) called the Kalam cosmological argument for the existence of God:

- Premise 1: Everything that begins to exist has a cause.
- Premise 2: The universe began to exist.
- Conclusion: The universe has a cause.

All conceptualization of time and space is in connection with the universe itself, but for the universe to begin to exist, there must be something outside of it (and greater than it) to cause it to begin. This cause is also beyond time and space. For such a cause/creation to occur, then what once did not exist (or what was once nothing) was caused to exist for the first time. In other words, something (or someone) caused something to come out of nothing. If anything describes a miracle, this is it.

Hebrews 11:3 takes this fact for granted: "By faith we understand that the universe was created by the word of God, so that what is seen was not made out of things that are visible." That is, only God, and not any preexisting material or anything else besides God, can account for what has been made. When this one thing is granted, miracles cannot be held as impossible.

But this is not the only kind of natural knowledge of God. While Romans 1 describes the external form of the natural knowledge of God, Romans 2 describes the internal form of the natural knowledge of God. This time, instead of looking at what is outside of us in creation, we look at what is inside of us: our conscience.

Romans 2:14–15 says, "For when Gentiles, who do not have the law, by nature do what the law requires, they are a law to themselves, even though they do not have the law. They show that the work of the law is written on their hearts, while their conscience also bears witness, and their conflicting thoughts accuse or even excuse them." C. S. Lewis referred to this truth from the Bible as the law of human nature, or the law of right and wrong. Even if people have never read the Bible or darkened the door of a church, they still have a conscience that tells them that some things are right and other things are wrong (whether they follow their conscience or not). This is evidence of a Lawgiver or higher authority. Here is another syllogism for the internal natural knowledge of God:

- Premise 1: If objective moral values exist, then these require a Lawgiver.
- Premise 2: Objective moral values *do* exist apart from anything people generate or do.
- Conclusion: A Lawgiver of objective moral values exists.

Now let's look at a hypothetical conversation between a Christian and a liberal Christian to see how we can discuss the natural knowledge of God. This conversation focuses on the external form of natural knowledge.

Liberal Christian: I believe in being a good person and I follow Jesus' teaching, but I cannot believe that Jesus is God in the flesh or that He bodily rose from the dead.

Christian: But you do believe that the universe and the world came into existence?

Liberal Christian: Of course I do.

Christian: So you believe that something or someone was powerful enough to create something out of nothing. That qualifies as a miracle. If God can create something out of nothing, how hard is it for Him to be raised from death?

But what if the liberal Christian does not grant the universe as having a beginning? What if he or she believes that the universe is eternal? The dialogue might then go like this:

Liberal Christian: Well, I would not say that the universe came into existence. I think it has always been.

Christian: Everyone is entitled to their opinion, but the biblical worldview is supported by both science and philosophy.

Liberal Christian: So you say.

Christian: I do, and I am not the only one. Science clearly observes that the universe is expanding, and the further away you go, the faster it expands. Measurable background radiation indicates that all of this commenced at a single point in time. The philosophical position simply states that while time could theoretically go infinitely forward, it cannot go infinitely back.

Liberal Christian: Why not?

Christian: Because if the universe went back infinitely, it would never arrive to the present. Both science and philosophy go against the idea of an eternal universe.

Liberal Christian: Are you saying you believe in a big bang?

Christian: Except for the inference that the beginning was chaotic or accidental, so I prefer "big bloom." That is, God knew exactly what He was doing when He said, "Let there be light" (Genesis 1:3). This describes a miracle, and if God could do this (and He did), then how easy would it be for Him to do the miracles associated with Jesus Christ, including His resurrection?

MIRACLES

In any discussion, we need to make sure we use correct terms and definitions. The philosopher David Hume (discussed above) defined miracles as violations of the laws of nature. But this is not what miracles are. The original Christian faith has never denied or ignored the laws of nature. Much to the contrary, because biblical Christianity believes that God is the almighty Creator, we believe the laws of nature were established by God, who created the natural order.

Therefore, we must use a better definition of *miracle*. God created and preserves the natural order with all its observable laws, such as the law of gravity. A miracle does not cancel the reality of natural laws but rather introduces a unique act by God alongside the natural laws, which do not change. A miracle is God's intervention within or interaction with the natural order, not transformation or change of natural order.

We can discuss God's intervention or interaction in two ways: top-down or bottom-up.

The top-down approach begins with the possibility of the existence of God, and this is exactly what the above discussion about the natural knowledge of God establishes. Once this is established, it is completely logical to assert that if God is God, then He is perfectly capable of intervening within and interacting with the natural order. He has both the power and authority to do so. Again, there is absolutely nothing illogical or unreasonable about this once the possibility of God's existence is established.

The bottom-up approach begins with something on earth (below) that testifies to the probability of God's existence, which is usually thought of as "up above" in heaven. In other words, we start with a miracle that has already happened here on earth. The best miracle to use in this approach is the bodily resurrection of the Lord Jesus Christ from the dead.

Using these ideas, a hypothetical conversation with a liberal Christian about miracles might go something like this:

Christian: **So why don't you believe in miracles?**

Liberal Christian: **Because miracles are violations of the laws of nature.**

Christian: If that were the case, then I would agree with you about miracles, but that is not what miracles are.

Liberal Christian: What would you call them?

Christian: The laws of nature are completely stable and inviolate, and miracles do not cancel these. Miracles are actually God's intervention within the created order or His interaction with the created order. The laws of nature are untouched.

Liberal Christian: I am not sure I follow.

Christian: Let's say you drop an apple from a second-story window, and the apple falls according to the law of gravity. But before the apple hits the ground, I reach out and grab the apple. My grabbing the apple does not violate the laws of nature. If God grabbed the apple, that would not be a violation of the laws of nature either, even if you see only that the apple never hit the ground and cannot see God catching it.

Liberal Christian: But I do not believe God does that.

Christian: I think you have good reason to reconsider. If God is real [refer to the above discussion on the natural knowledge of God], then it is completely in His ability to intervene and interact. Besides, there is another good reason to believe He can catch that apple.

Liberal Christian: Which is?

Christian: There is historical evidence—and a lot of it—that God has already conducted a miracle right here on earth.

THE RESURRECTION OF CHRIST

Liberal Christianity flatly denies the resurrection of the Lord Jesus Christ. Why? The same reason we just discussed: because it is a miracle and miracles do not happen. When this discussion arises, we do not need to be on the defensive. Instead, we should feel free to ask questions, as in the example below.

Christian: So what do *you* think happened regarding Christ's resurrection, which is so strongly attested to in the four Gospels and other historical sources that acknowledge the strong belief that Jesus was alive on earth after He died?

Liberal Christian: Well, one of the leading theories is that Jesus' disciples stole His body from the tomb.

Christian: But why would they do such a thing?

Liberal Christian: Because they were disciples of Jesus. Their whole identity and newly found status were bound up in being disciples of Jesus. They were essentially trying to guard their reputations.

Christian: So you are saying that the disciples stole Jesus' body to somehow benefit from their deception?

Liberal Christian: Exactly.

Christian: For many reasons, that argument doesn't make sense.

Jesus was crucified because of a false charge of sedition against the Roman Empire, which means that His disciples would automatically be associated with this false accusation. That means the disciples were automatically in trouble and would have made it worse by not denouncing Christ. Why would they want to remain in this threatening and compromised position?

By stealing the body, they would be volunteering to be hated by the enemies of Jesus Christ. They would be signing up to be persecuted. Not only would they not gain anything from this deception, but most would, in fact, also lose everything on account of this deception! Reliable church tradition tells us that all of the apostles were martyred except John, who was exiled.

Stealing Jesus' body would also mean that the apostles were going against everything Jesus stood for, including telling the truth and hating falsehood.

Finally, if they had stolen the body, then almost all of them were strong enough in the face of martyrdom to die for an incredible lie.

THE BIBLE AS TRUSTWORTHY SOURCE

The resurrection of Jesus is also backed up by the high integrity, trustworthiness, and reliability of the Word of God. The Holy Scriptures are considered both inspired and inerrant by biblical Christianity for good reasons:

- The Scriptures have strong internal evidence. In other words, they are consistent within themselves. Any apparent contradictions of Holy Scripture are just that—only apparent. Most contradictions can be explained immediately, but if you hear one that seems legitimate, take it to your pastor. He can help you dig deeper into your Bible to understand how Scripture is consistent. In fact, many examples demonstrate that the books of the Holy Bible are consistent and complementary. For example, the four Gospels of Matthew, Mark, Luke, and John have impressive unique vantage points, meaning that they are not identical. The differences between the accounts, rather than being contradictory, are complementary and give us a fuller picture of the historical events.

- The Scriptures also have strong external evidence. External disciplines such as history, geography, and archeology demonstrate the accuracy of Holy Scriptures, which is why some people say that archaeology is the Bible's best friend.

- The Scriptures have strong bibliographical evidence. Thousands of ancient manuscripts of the New Testament exist. With so many ancient manuscripts, one might expect inconsistencies in the major teachings of the Christian faith, such as the miraculous events. Instead, we find amazing verification and confirmation of the historical events among the thousands of ancient manuscripts.

But there is more to the high integrity, trustworthiness, and reliability of the Word of God, especially in the New Testament. The New Testament documents that record the resurrection of Jesus Christ have two important characteristics: they are early and based on eyewitness accounts.

First, the proclamation of Christ's resurrection occurred early in time—within twenty-five years of the event itself. This means that the clear historical assertion and teaching of Christ's resurrection cannot be treated as mythological. Myths have a vast amount of time separating the record of the event from the actual event. But the New Testament was written soon after the events occurred. The authors were proclaiming something that would certainly have been challenged by contemporaneous enemies and naysayers of the events.

Second, this record of the resurrection of Jesus Christ is backed up by eyewitnesses, and not only a few! Hundreds of people witnessed these events, as it says in 1 Corinthians 15:3–8. As most people know, having eyewitness testimony is the standard test for reliability in a court of law. Once a claim is made, it must be confirmed by eyewitnesses giving consistent testimony. In the case of the disciples, this eyewitness testimony was combined with their willingness to die for their testimony—not to mention the amazing life transformation of the disciples, even those once skeptical, after Jesus rose from death. Based on this, the evidence for the risen Lord Jesus Christ is impeccable.

WHAT IS AT STAKE?

Because liberal Christianity undermines the Word of God itself, it gravely affects the Means of Grace, the Word, and the Sacraments. Compromising the Word of God also compromises the Gospel as it is proclaimed and administered through those Means. In other words, people are cut off from the Means of Grace, from their connection to the grace of God in Christ.

Romans 1:16–17 states, "For I am not ashamed of the gospel, for it is the power of God for salvation to everyone who believes, to the Jew first and also to the Greek. For in it the righteousness of God is revealed from faith for faith, as it is written, 'The righteous shall live by faith.'"

The phrase "from faith for faith" means that God's saving righteousness in Jesus Christ is given to people through the Word of God. The first "faith" in the phrase is the Word of God: the objective faith, "the faith that was once for all delivered to the saints" (Jude 3). We should never compromise the Word of God, this objective faith, because without it we would lose the Holy Spirit's work through the Word to create subjective faith (the second faith in the passage), which trusts in the Gospel from the heart.

Through this gift of faith (Ephesians 2:8), which comes to us through the pure and uncompromised Word of God (Romans 10:17), saving faith holds to Jesus Christ, who overcame sin and death. This is why we must never compromise the Bible.

BIBLICAL CHRISTIANITY MEETS OUR REAL NEEDS

Biblical Christianity acknowledges the real problems of humanity: sin and death. While liberal Christianity downplays these ultimate threats, biblical Christianity meets them head-on. Because of sin and death, people—real people in real life—live with guilt (knowing they have done wrong), shame (believing that something is wrong with themselves), and fear (because no one has a real answer to our greatest threat, death).

Biblical Christianity provides the only real answer to these enemies of humanity. Jesus Christ is God in flesh who came into the world to do something about our sin and death. As true man, He was able to suffer the penalty of sin, as He accepted our guilt upon Himself. As true God, He had the right and authority to forgive the sins of all people He created—every single one of us.

Most important, after Jesus dealt with our sin through His life lived to keep God's Law for us and His atoning death on the cross, which covered our sins with His life-giving blood, He rose from the dead. Jesus Christ has done something about death, our worst enemy.

And this is what God's inspired and inerrant Word makes clear for us: "Now Jesus did many other signs in the presence of the disciples, which are not written in this book; but these are written so that you may believe that Jesus is the Christ, the Son of God, and that by believing you may have life in His name" (John 20:30–31).